"We Are Not Monkeys!"

Written by
Jill Atkins

This book is about **apes**. When is it a monkey and when is it an ape?

One way apes are different from monkeys is that apes have no tails. Most monkeys have tails.

No tail: it's an ape

Tail: it's a monkey

Many apes inhabit the rainforests of Africa.

The biggest ape is the gorilla. The dominant male is called a silverback, because of the silver fur down his back. If he stands on his hind legs, he is as tall as a man – but he is a lot stronger than the strongest man!

The rest of the troop is his family. There are about ten gorillas in a troop.

Did you know that a baby gorilla is called an infant? Infant gorillas drink their mum's milk.

They stay with her until they are about three years old. They cling to her fur as she travels through the forest.

An infant with his mother

Gorillas spend a lot of time in trees, but they spend time on the ground too.

They make a nest on the ground, where they sleep at night.

Gorillas have wide mouths and sharp teeth.

They eat bamboo shoots, roots, tree bark, seeds and insects. They drink water from rivers and streams.

Chimpanzees are African apes too. They look really small beside a gorilla.

Chimpanzees live in a bigger troop than gorillas. They can travel fast on their feet and fists, and they're very clever.

Male chimps sometimes want to display their power. They scream and stamp their feet again and again to scare their enemy.

But they like to have fun too. They sometimes behave like humans, by kissing, hugging and tickling each other!

Have you heard of a **bonobo**?

Bonobos are African apes too. They are related to chimpanzees, but they are much smaller.

Bonobos are very shy and like to hide in the forest. But they enjoy playing and hugging and kissing, just like chimps.

A bonobo sometimes walks on its hind legs, carrying an infant on its back.

Gibbons are the smallest of the African apes.

They have very long arms, which they use to swing through the trees. They can walk on their hind legs too and they're the most acrobatic of all the apes.

Gibbons communicate by a kind of singing.

Orangutans are apes too, but they don't live in Africa. They live in places like Borneo.

Like the gibbon, they spend most of their lives swinging from tree to tree.

An orangutan's arms are much longer than its legs! Their hands and feet are like human hands, with four fingers and a thumb.

They use their hands and feet for climbing and gripping, as well as for eating.

Sadly, there are people who cut down the forests where these apes live.

Many apes will die because they have lost their habitat. This means they are endangered.

It's good that there are other people who work hard to protect these animals.